SHIPS AND SEAFARERS

A chronological study from the Romans to modern times

Richard Dawson

A Piccolo Original
Piccolo Books

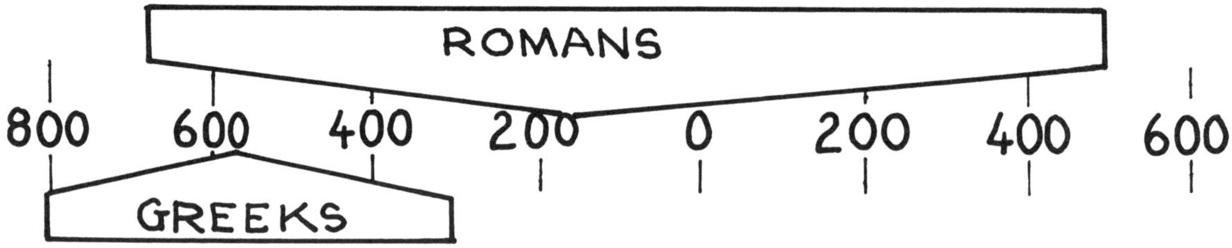

THE GREEKS

The Greeks had the lightest and most stylish of all ships in the ancient world. Greek coastal traders sailed between the different Greek islands and mainland harbours, never leaving sight of land. All ships had one large square sail: this was the only type of sail used in the ancient world.

The cargo was loaded into the bottom of the ship.
Look carefully at the picture, how did the crew move about the ship without treading on the cargo? ____________________

On the bow of many ships there were two painted eyes.
What do you think they were for?

____

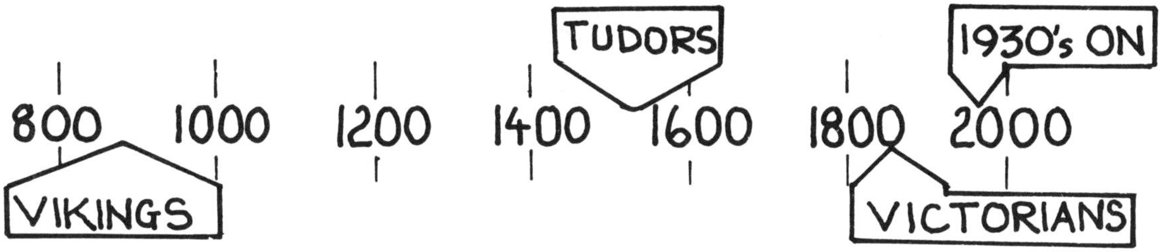

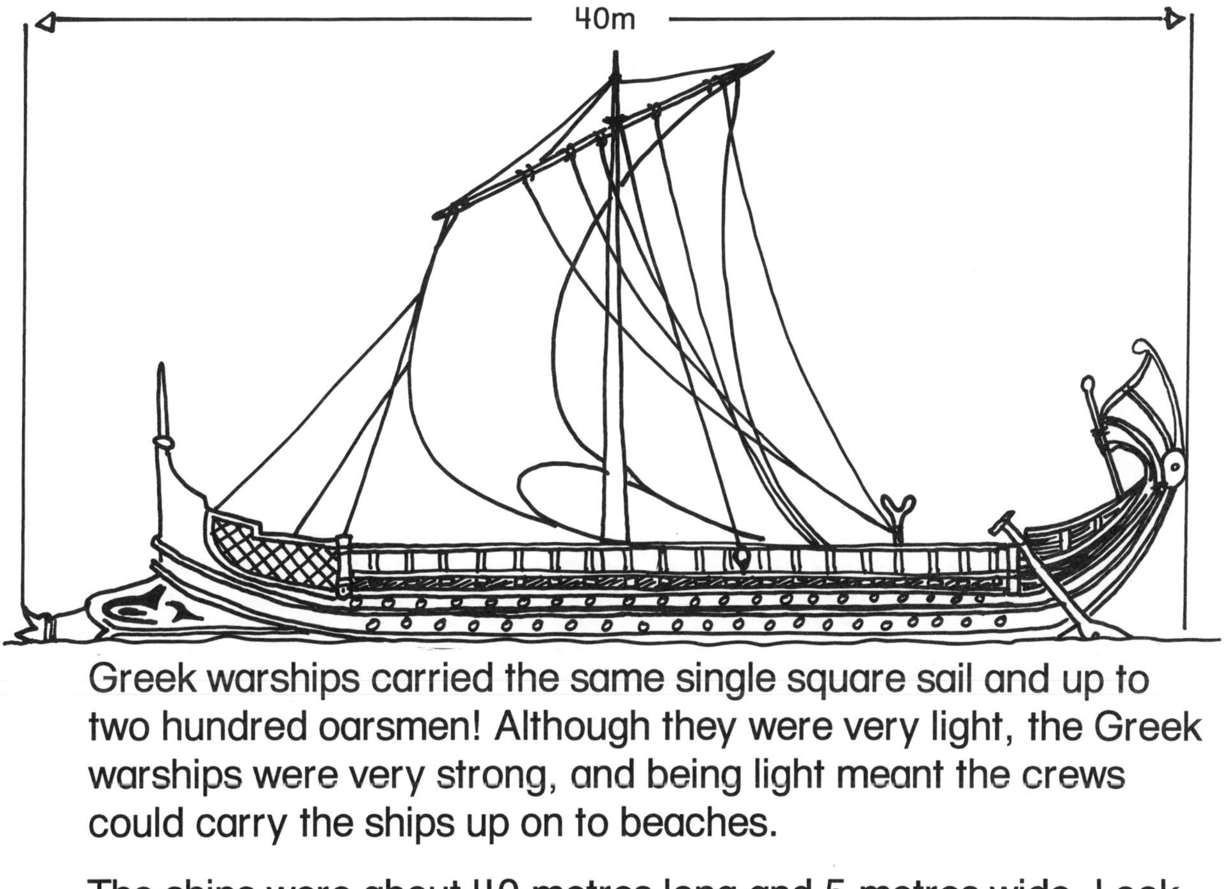

Greek warships carried the same single square sail and up to two hundred oarsmen! Although they were very light, the Greek warships were very strong, and being light meant the crews could carry the ships up on to beaches.

The ships were about 40 metres long and 5 metres wide. Look at the bow. What do you think the pointed end was used for?

The trireme was believed to have three rows of oars. The oars would have been 5 metres long so that they could reach the water and needed more than one man to move them.

Some people say that a trireme was so called because it needed three men to each oar – not because it had three rows of oars!

The Greeks were always drawn to the mysteries of the sea. Greece is a mountainous country and it has never been possible to grow enough food to support the entire population. The ancient Greeks turned to the riches of the sea in great numbers as fishermen, sea traders, fighters and pirates.

As early as 450 BC the Greeks began to have ideas that the world was not flat but round. A Greek mathematician, Ptolemy (AD 150) plotted lines of latitude and longitude to all territories known to the Greeks.

What is a line of latitude?

____

What is a line of longitude?

____

How were these useful to the seamen?

____

____

____

____

THE ROMANS

The Romans copied the Greek ship designs. They did add their own ideas; the merchant ships almost always had a swan-necked stern and the warships had a 'castle' construction on the desk. Both ships had extra sails.

Draw either a Roman merchant ship or a warship! Use the pictures of the Greek ships to help.

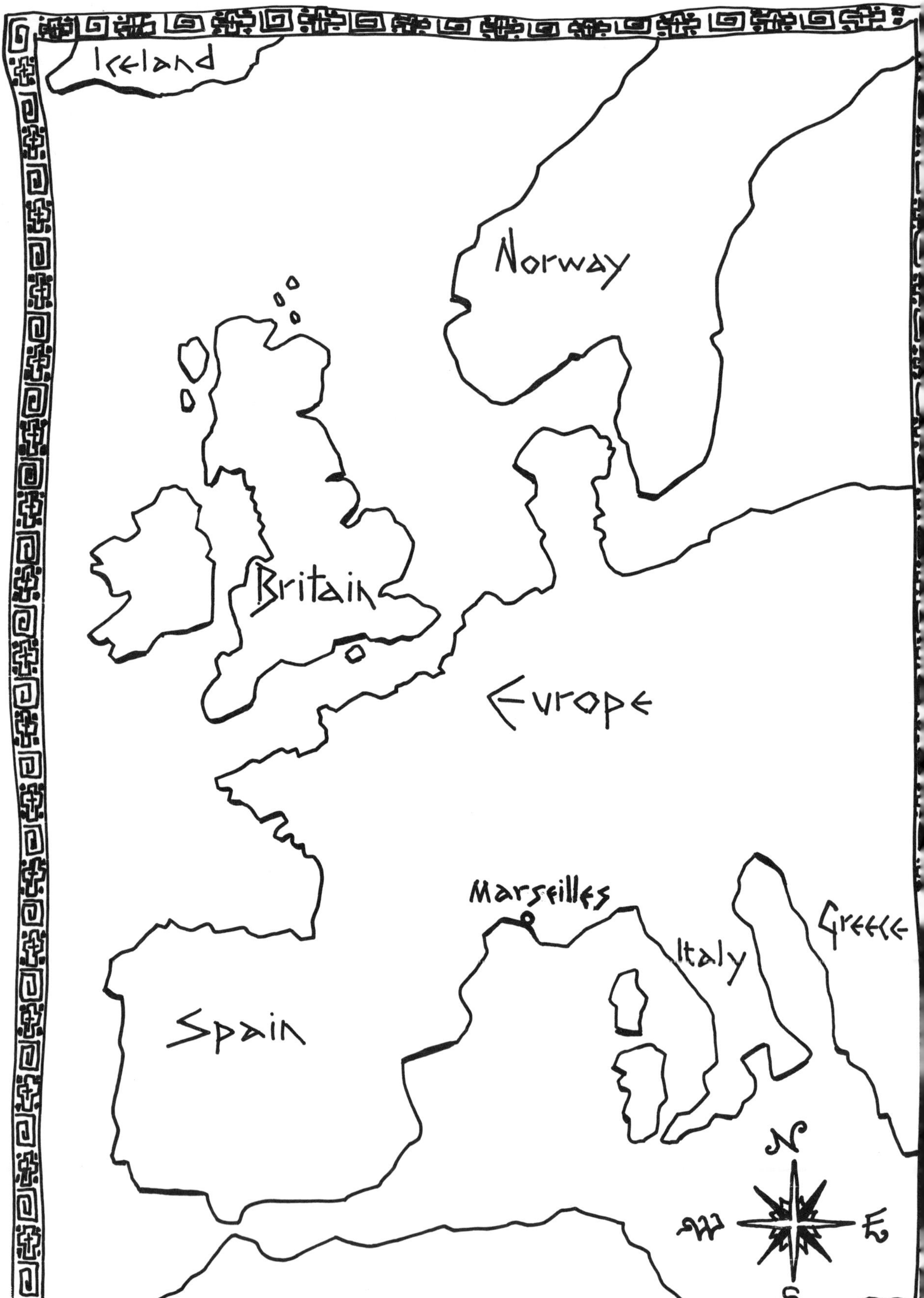
Iceland
Norway
Britain
Europe
Marseilles
Spain
Italy
Greece
N
W
E
S

Round Britain Tour

In 325 BC, the Greek astronomer, Pytheas, made a famous voyage. Although he was a Greek, Pytheas was born and lived in Marseilles (in France) which was at that time a Greek colony.

He sailed from Marseilles up the east coast of Britain to an island he called 'Thule' and back down the west coast of Britain to Marseilles. At this time the Phoenicians traded extensively in this area, mainly for the metal, tin. Pytheas was trying to trade for tin himself and was looking for the tin mines.

Plot in Pytheas' route around Britain.

On his return to Marseilles, Pytheas described the British people as being 'very friendly'.

The Romans not only sailed on voyages of discovery but also sent in their armies to capture the lands! By 138 AD, the Roman Empire extended all over Europe to include Spain, France, Italy, Greece, Germany, Austria, Switzerland, Portugal and England. The Empire also covered the northern coastlands of Africa.

Colour in the Roman Empire – purple!

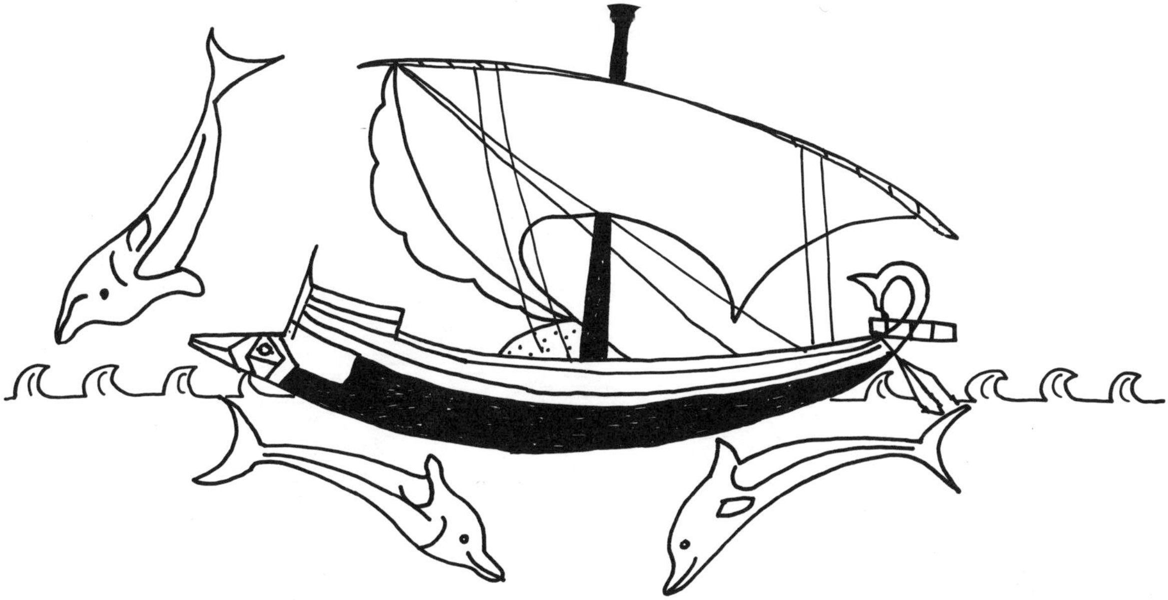

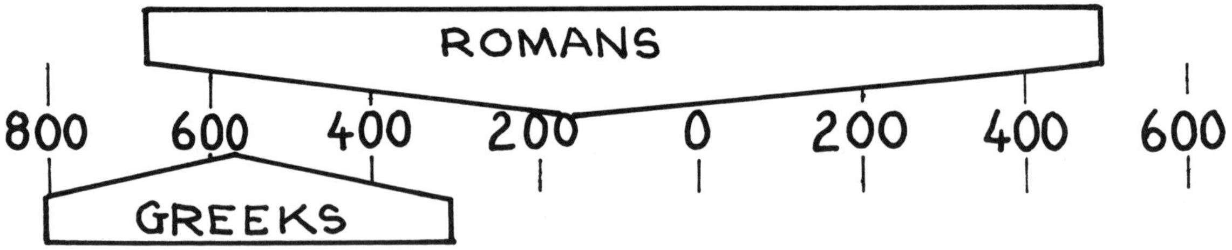

THE VIKINGS

Vikings came from Scandinavia – those countries we now call Norway, Sweden, Denmark and Finland.

In 793 AD Viking longships landed on the island of Lindisfarne, off the coast of Northumberland, and attacked and robbed the monastery that was there.

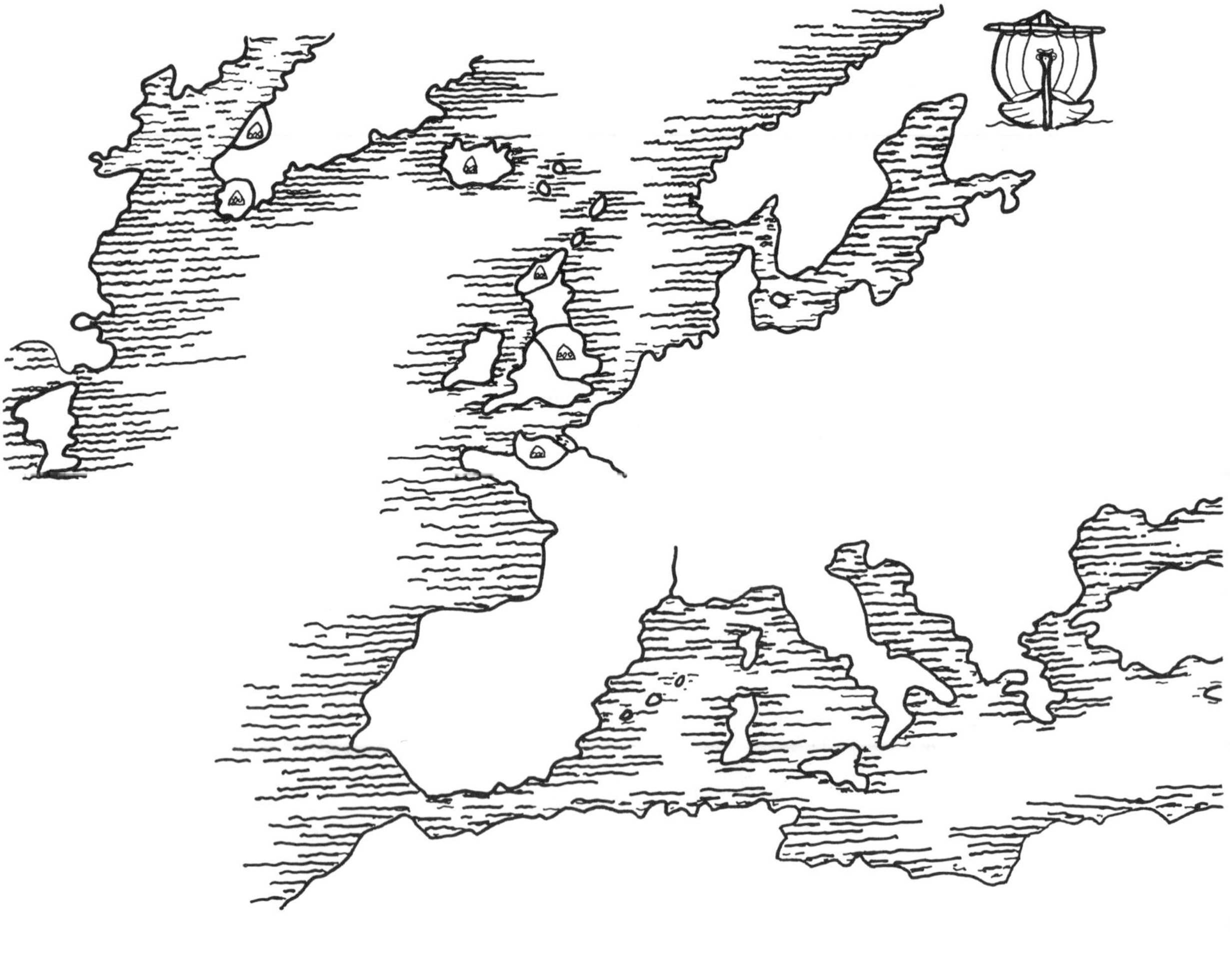

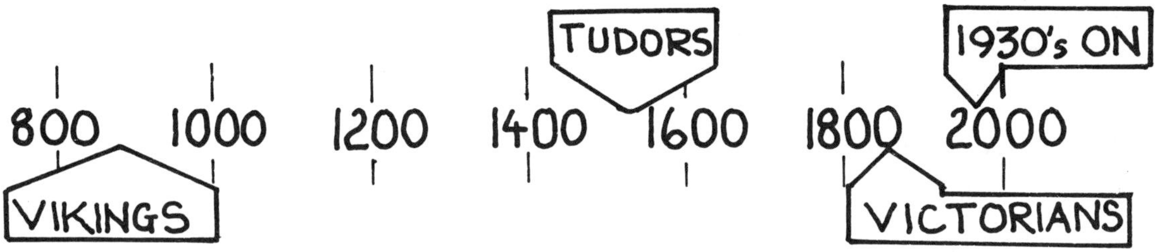

The Vikings were great sailors and fierce fighters! Here are some of the places they sailed to and raided over the next two hundred years.

Iceland

Lindisfarne

York

London – they sailed up the Thames

Paris in France

Dublin in Ireland

Gibraltar

Salerno in Italy

Jerez in Spain

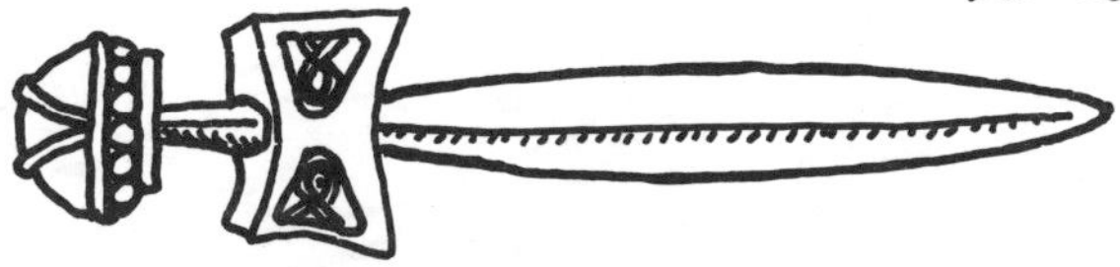

Istanbul in Turkey

Athens in Greece

Lisbon in Portugal

Newfoundland in Canada

Mark all the places the Vikings sailed to and raided on their expeditions and plot a route from Stockholm in Sweden, where the Vikings might have sailed from.

Vikings settled and built villages where the helmets can be seen on the map. Colour these settlements green.

A Viking Longship

Almost 30 metres long . . .
Speeds up to 15 mph.

The terror of the seas!

A cross section of the hull.

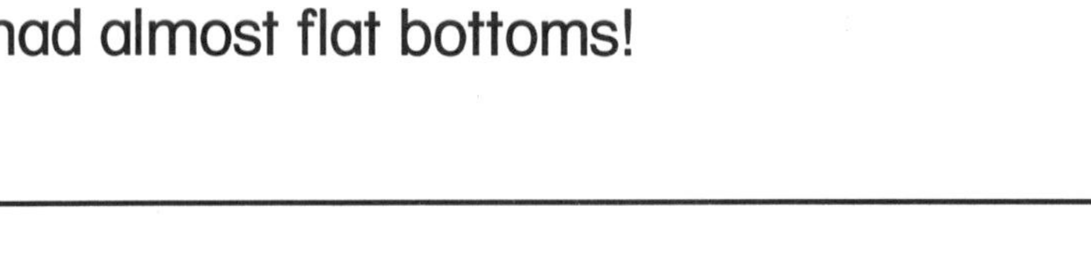

The boats had almost flat bottoms!

Why? ______________________________

Make a model boat from a polystyrene tray

Fix a paper sail in position and float your boat . . .

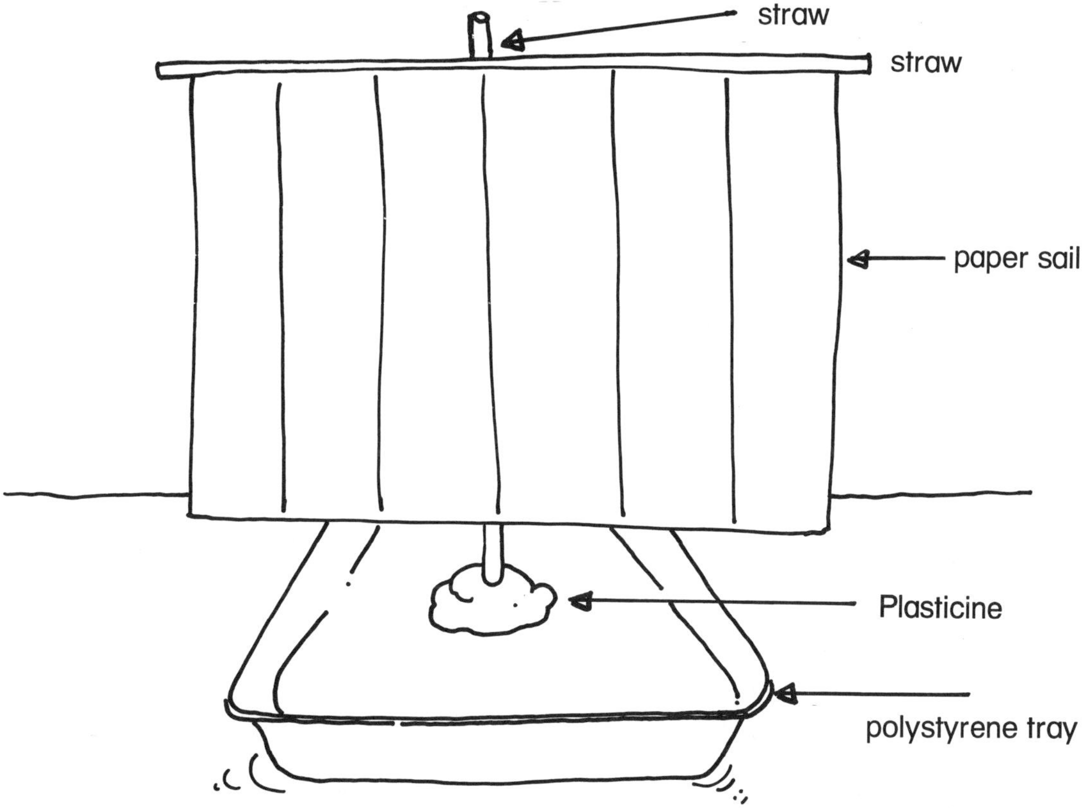

Blow behind your boat . . . what happens?

___

___

Blow to the side of your boat . . . what happens?

___

___

When might the Vikings use their oars?

___

___

The Battle of Gibraltar

In about 880 AD two Viking chiefs, Hastein and Bjorm Ironside sailed up the river Seine in France. With a fleet of over sixty ships they plundered their way to Paris, then decided to head south for Spain.

The Spanish were waiting for the raiders and after a hard fought battle, with the loss of two ships, the Vikings made off along the coast of north Africa looking for slaves, and then on to the coast of France.

Hastein had heard about the rich city of Rome and, eager for more treasure, the Vikings set sail once again. Early one morning as the sun rose, a sharp-eyed look-out saw a marble city glinting on the hillside. Surely they had reached Rome?

The Vikings raided. The huge city walls held back the raiders, but by pretending Hastein had been killed in the battle and needed to be buried, the Vikings tricked their way in. It was not Rome though, it was the Italian city of Luna, and the Vikings were furious. They slaughtered as many people as they could find and set fire to the city. This atrocity ended their expedition, and they set off back to Scandinavia.

As they passed Gibraltar a strong Spanish fleet attacked and savagely beat them, sinking all but twenty ships. The Vikings limped on back to their homeland, thus ending a four year reign of terror.

Play your own 'Battle of Gibraltar' game

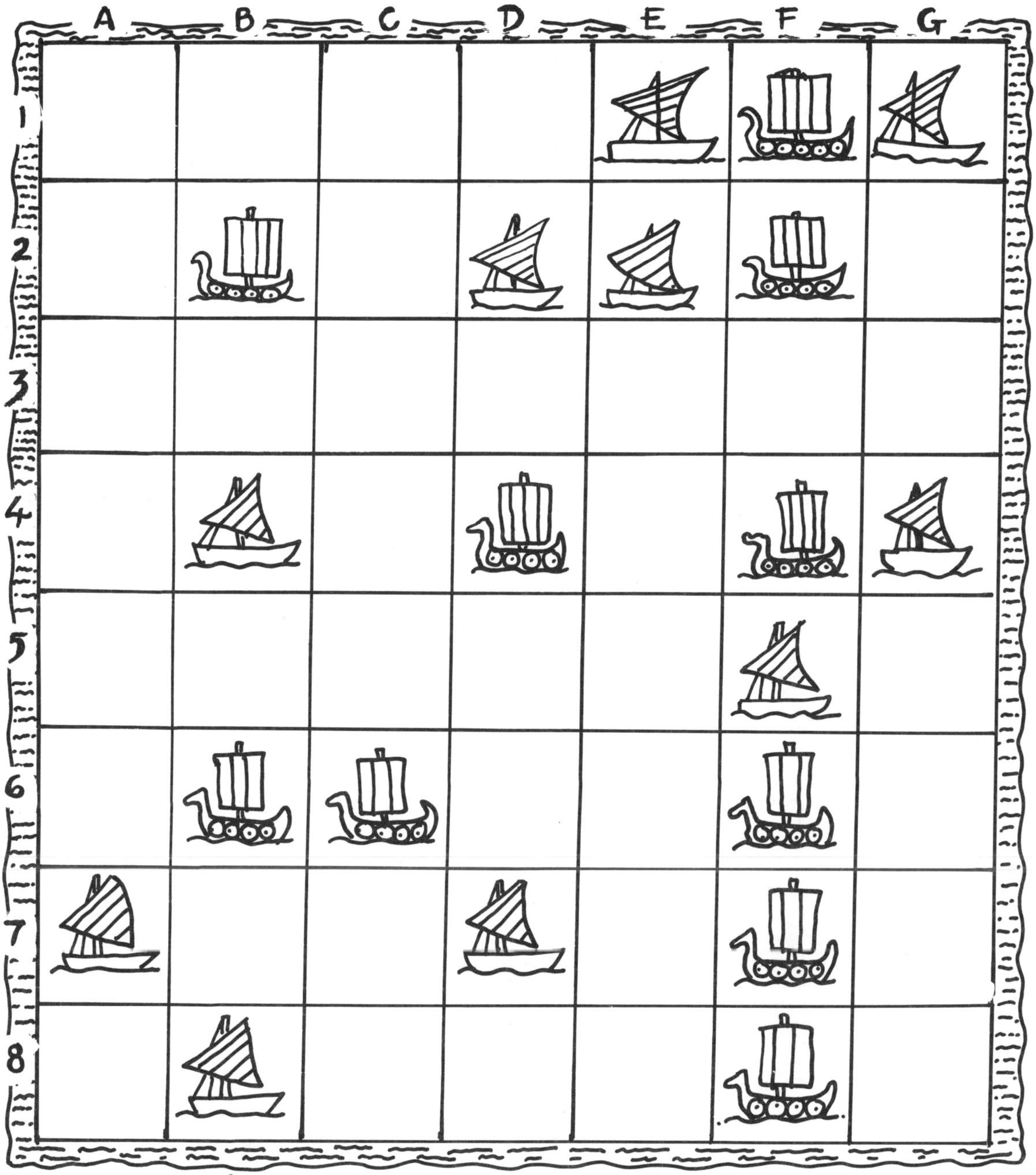

 Viking

 Spanish

Ask someone to call out grid references e.g. 4C. Mark an X in the square. Continue until one side is wiped out!
Who wins your battle? ______________________________

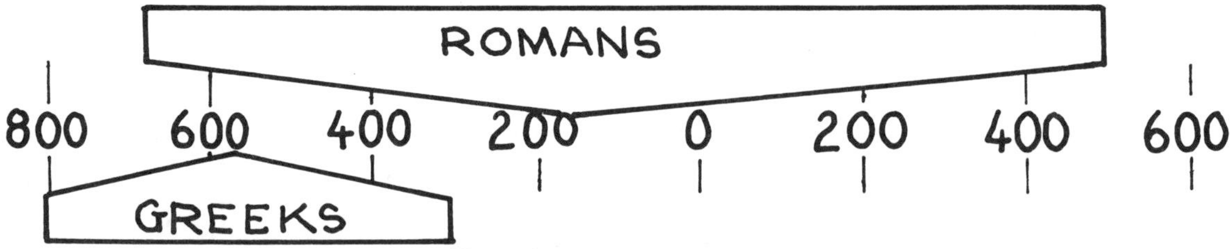

In 1577 Francis Drake left Plymouth on a journey that was to last three years.

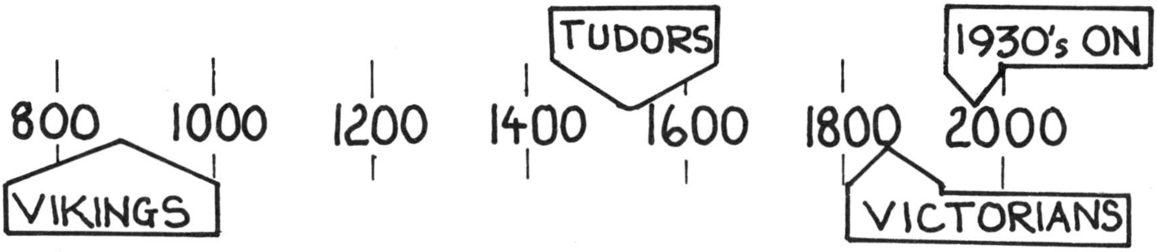

THE TUDORS

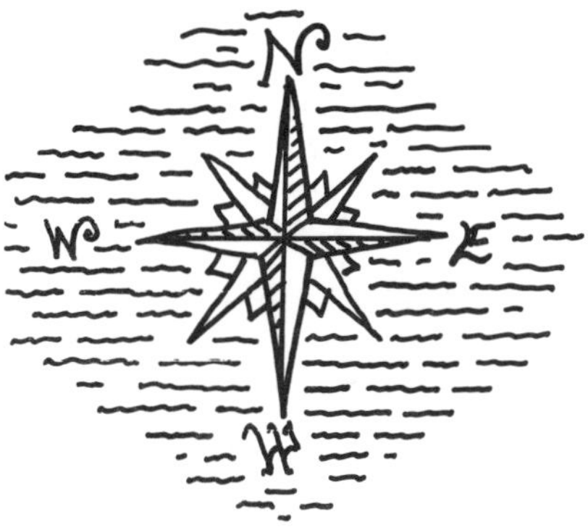

On the command of Queen Elizabeth I, Francis Drake sailed from Plymouth to Cape Verdi Island, off the west African coast. Here the crew stocked up with fruit and coconuts for their long journey towards the Magellan Straits.

No one on board was prepared for the calm of the windless Doldrums, or, by contrast, the storms as they battled for sixteen days to pass through the Magellan Straits. Drake then headed north along the west coast of South America filling the holds of his ship with bounty seized from Spanish treasure ships.

Continuing northwards, in June 1579 Drake and his crew landed in California, and there they rested and prepared the ship for the long journey back to England. Several more Spanish settlements were raided, swelling the treasure seized to over £20 million!

From California the ship sailed across the Pacific to the East Indies where the crew rested at Moluccas. Adding spices to their cargo, they sailed on across the Indian Ocean around the Cape of Good Hope, then back up the coast of Africa and Europe to Plymouth.

Plot Drake's route on the map opposite.

Find out the name of Francis Drake's ship. ____________________

What differences are there between a Viking longboat and a Tudor sailing ship?

What improvements have been made to the Tudor sailing ship?

Colour in those things introduced to England by the Tudor explorers.

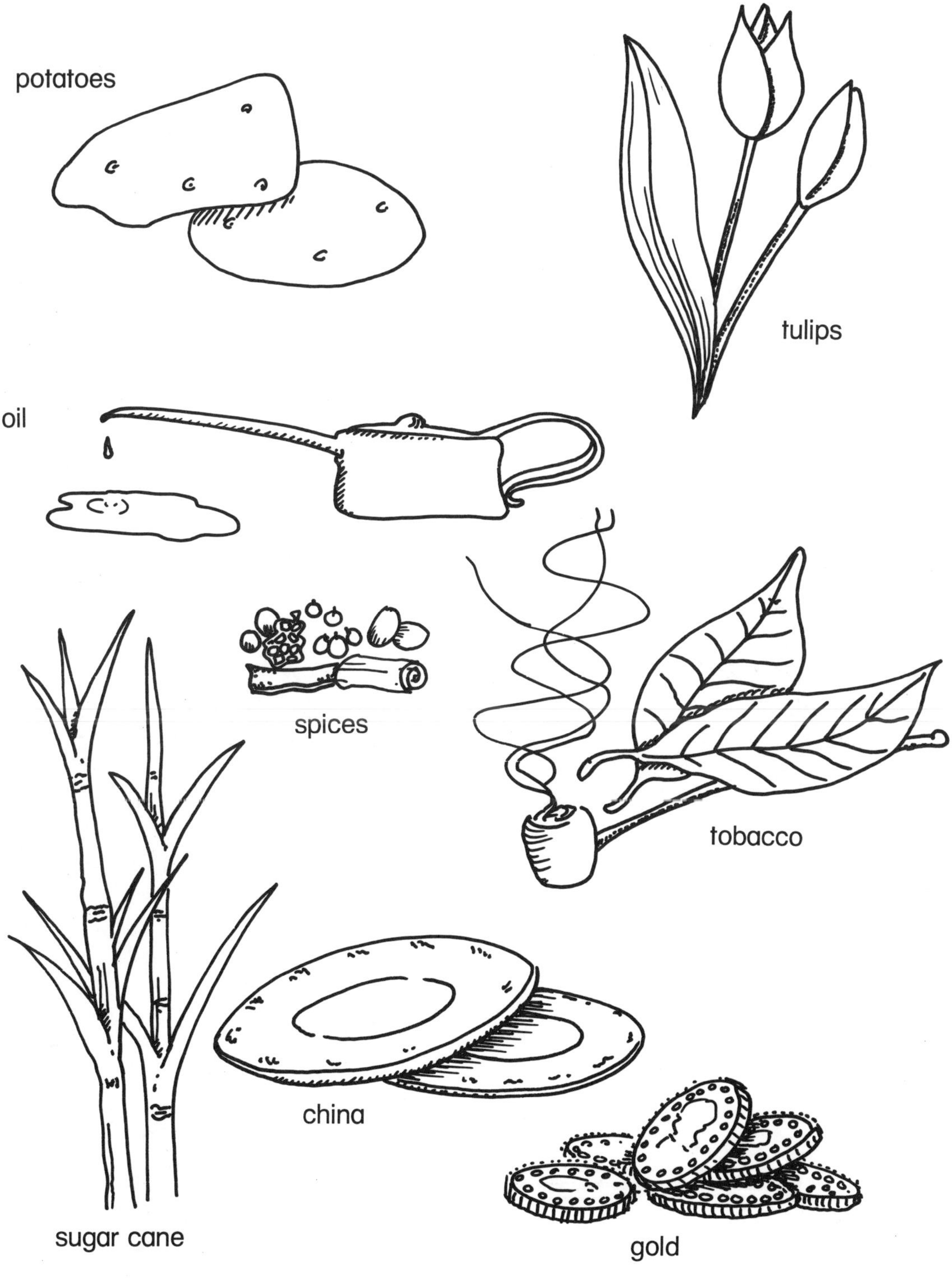

The Spanish grew tired of Drake's attacks on their treasure ships and decided to punish England.

In the summer of 1588 King Philip of Spain put together a fleet of about 130 ships called the ________ ___________.

What does the second word mean?

____

Colour in the weapons that might have been used in the battle.

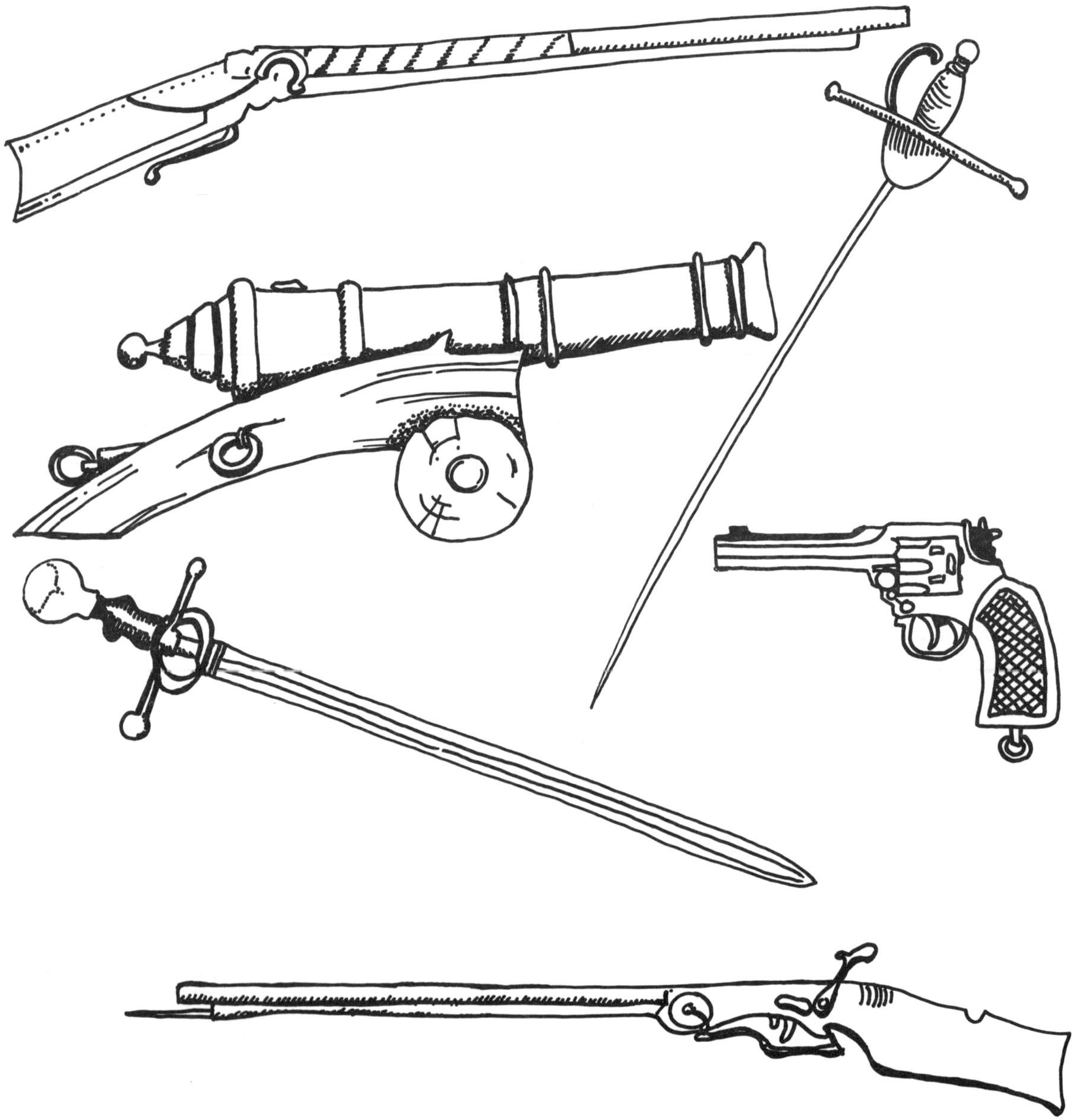

Have your own Battle of the Armada!

Place a 10p coin at the bottom of the page and strike it with your hand. Aim for the Spanish ships but don't sink your own!

Who won your battle? ______________________________

Why? ______________________________

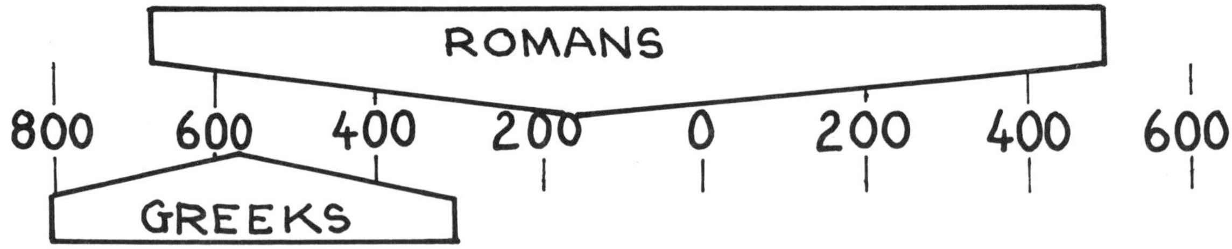

THE VICTORIANS

One of the many reasons that men sailed the seas in Victorian times was to catch whales. Whales provided many essential household goods in the 1800s and lots of money could be made by successful crews. Many kinds of ships were built for the purpose of whaling; here are some of them . . .

A top sail schooner

A brig

A bark

A three-masted schooner

If you look carefully at the ships you will notice that each carries a number of small boats hanging on the side. They are not lifeboats so what do you think they were used for?

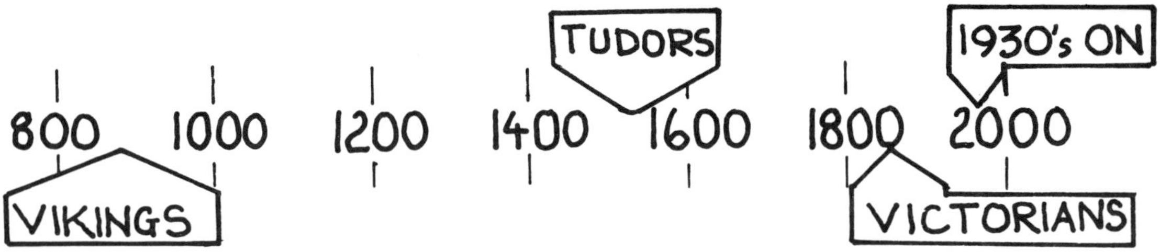

Whales were caught for their blubber, baleen, bone, and, the rarest whale product of all, ambergris – ambergris is worth its weight in gold!

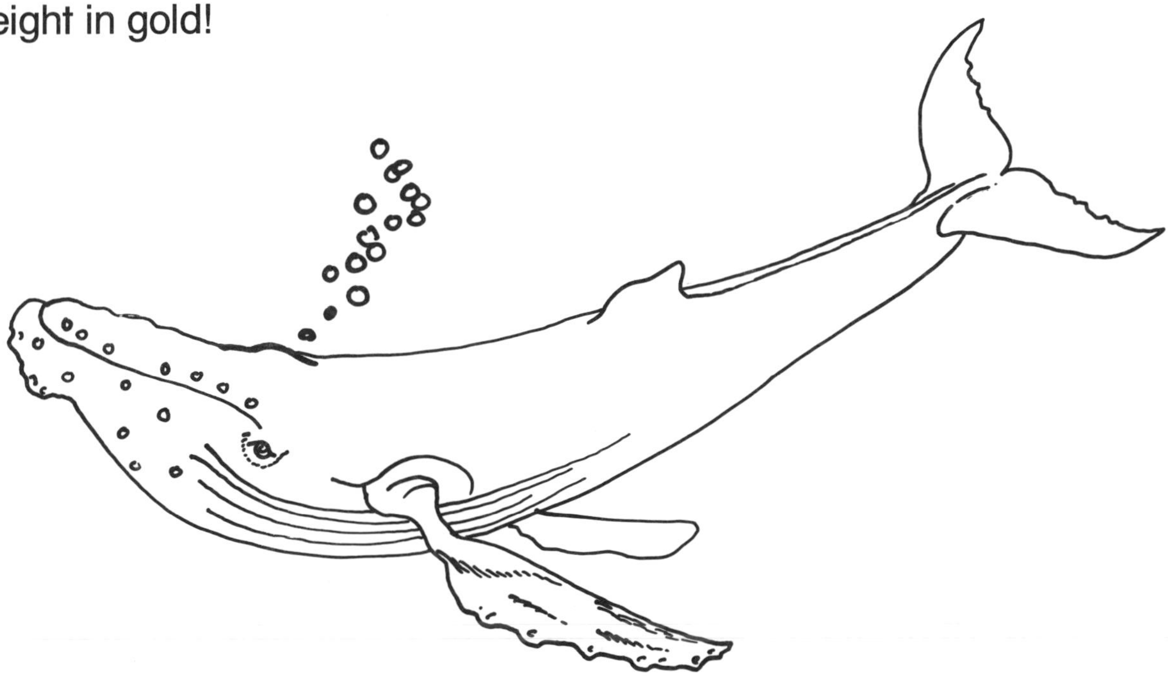

What do you think the Victorians used the whale products for?

Baleen ______________________________

Bone ______________________________

Blubber ______________________________

Ambergris ______________________________

Only one of these has any real value today, which one? __________

Why are the other products no longer of any value? __________

____

Until the early nineteenth century all ships were powered by sail . . . then things began to change.

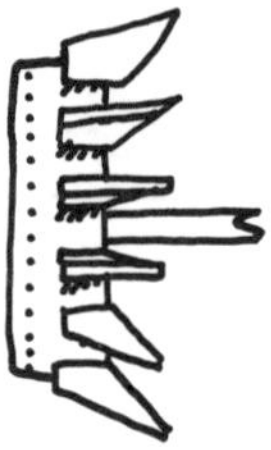

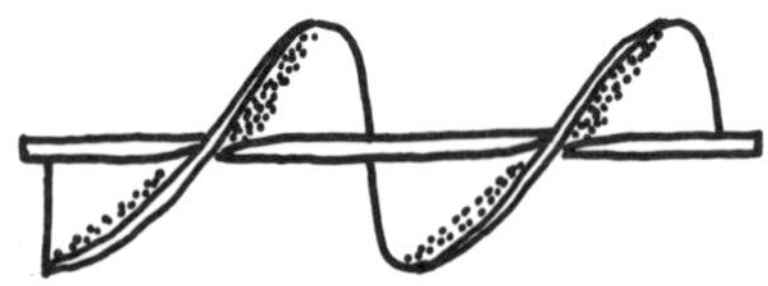

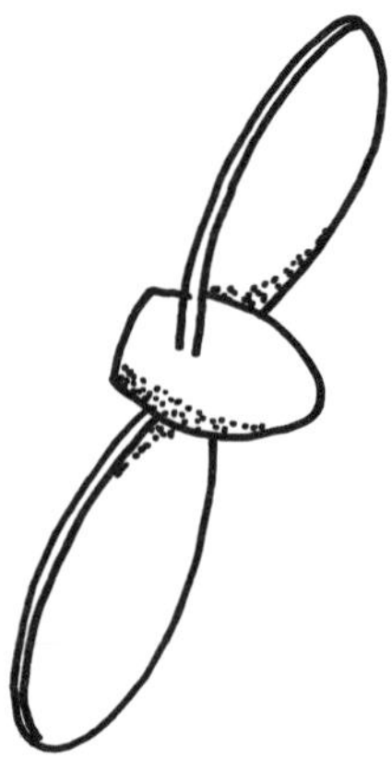

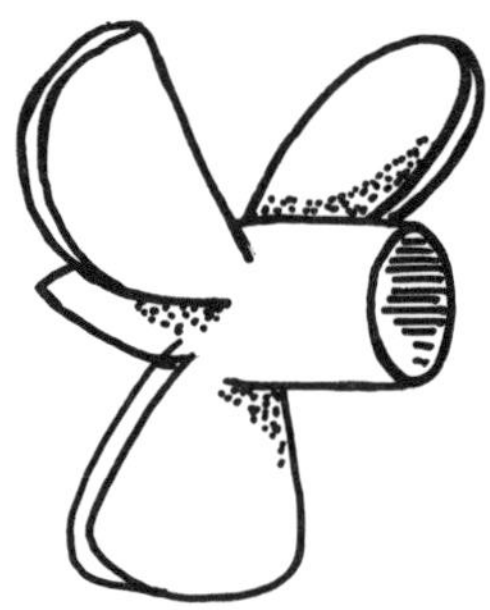

Paddle wheels were fixed to the sides or to the stern of ships and were driven by steam engines. They turned, and pulled the ships through the water.

The Archimedean screw was fixed to the stern of the boat and, driven by a steam engine, pushed the boat through the water.

Propellers were turned by the ship's engines: the curved blades 'bit' the water and pushed the ship through the water. The two-bladed propeller had to have long blades to be effective and the pressure of the water soon broke the blades.

Today propellers are made of very strong steel and have three or four blades.

What made these Victorian ships go?

The *Great Britain*
sail/steam
paddle/propeller

The *Charlotte Dundas*
sail/steam
paddle/propeller

The *Clermont*
sail/steam
paddle/propeller

The *Adriatic*
sail/steam
paddle/propeller

The *Savannah*
sail/steam
paddle/propeller

A Daring rescue by a Darling girl!

As ships no longer had to rely on the wind for power, ships sailed in all weather – often in bad storms. In 1838 the Forfarshire, a paddle steamer, was on a voyage from Hull to Dundee.

The ship's boiler had started leaking and was losing power – when a storm blew up, the engine stopped altogether! The ship started to drift towards the Longstone lighthouse off the Northumberland coast – a warning of rocks under the sea – and suddenly the Forfarshire crashed, and split in two.

Many passengers and crew members were swept away but eight men and one woman clung to the wreck. In the early morning the survivors scrambled on to a rock and were seen by the daughter of the lighthouse keeper – Grace Darling. She called her father and between the two of them they launched their fishing boat in the stormy sea. Mr Darling could not manage the boat on his own so Grace picked up the oars and started to row.

How many journeys did the boat have to make to rescue all the people if it could only carry five people at a time?

This rescue became very famous and it was realized that a sea rescue service ought to be formed. It was not long before the Royal National Lifeboat Institution – RNLI – began.

A Victorian Sea Search

A	G	R	E	A	T	W	H	A	L	E	A
B	R	C	D	E	B	F	G	H	P	I	M
J	A	K	L	M	R	N	O	P	A	Q	B
R	C	S	T	U	I	V	W	S	D	X	E
Y	E	Z	A	B	T	C	D	C	D	E	R
F	D	S	T	E	A	M	G	H	L	H	G
I	A	J	B	R	I	G	K	O	E	L	R
M	R	N	O	P	N	Q	R	O	S	T	I
U	L	O	N	G	S	T	O	N	E	V	S
W	I	X	Y	S	A	I	L	E	Z	A	B
C	N	B	L	U	B	B	E	R	D	E	F
G	G	H	P	R	O	P	E	L	L	E	R

Can you find all eleven words/names?

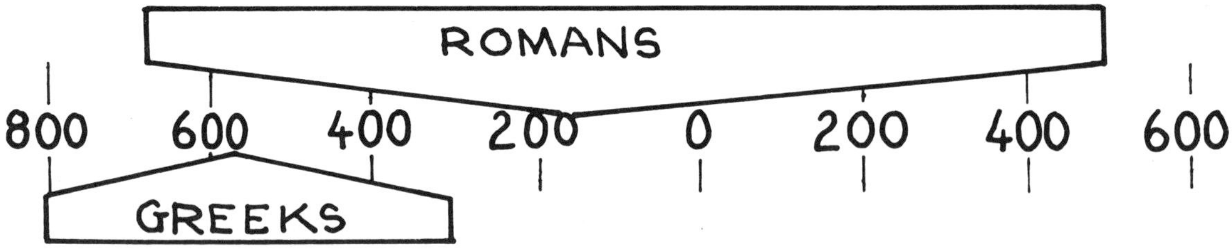

THE 1930s ONWARD

The early 1900s saw the heyday of Atlantic liner travel. Liners were huge passenger ships that accommodated every luxury. Many great ships were built, including the Titanic – believed to be the world's first unsinkable ship.

Sailing from England to the USA with over 2000 passengers on its maiden voyage, the ship hit an iceberg and sank! The 'unsinkable' Titanic went down and 1513 people lost their lives.

How did the iceberg sink the ship? Draw in the rest of the iceberg.

About fifty years ago there were up to sixty liners on the regular Atlantic run – today there are none! Why not?

____

____

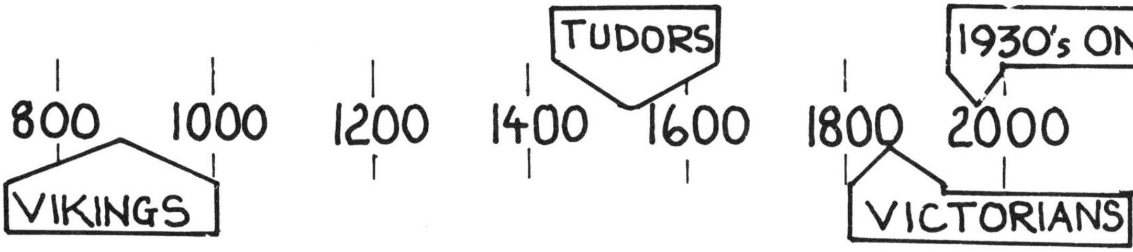

Being surrounded by water has always been of great benefit to the British Isles. However, during 1939 when World War Two broke out, food and supplies had to be brought in by ship, and the enemy quickly recognized how it could make life hard in Britain. Over 5000 merchant ships – ships that carry supplies – were sunk in the war. Britain built many warships to protect its fleets and coast; many great battles were fought, some won, some lost.

What type of Navy vessels are these?

tatpihsleb

reusicr

mebsurina

tfriaacr rrracie

The sea has always held a wealth of food. All man's powers of ingenuity have been brought into action to reap its harvest; special ships have been designed and built.

The 1950s was the era of the fishing industry. Fish were mainly caught in two ways . . .

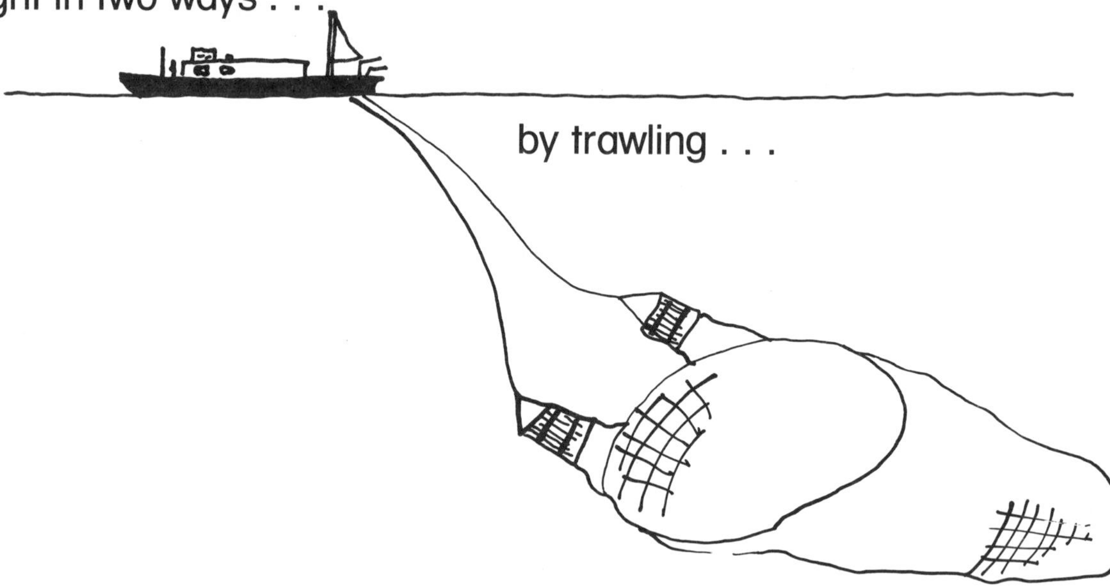

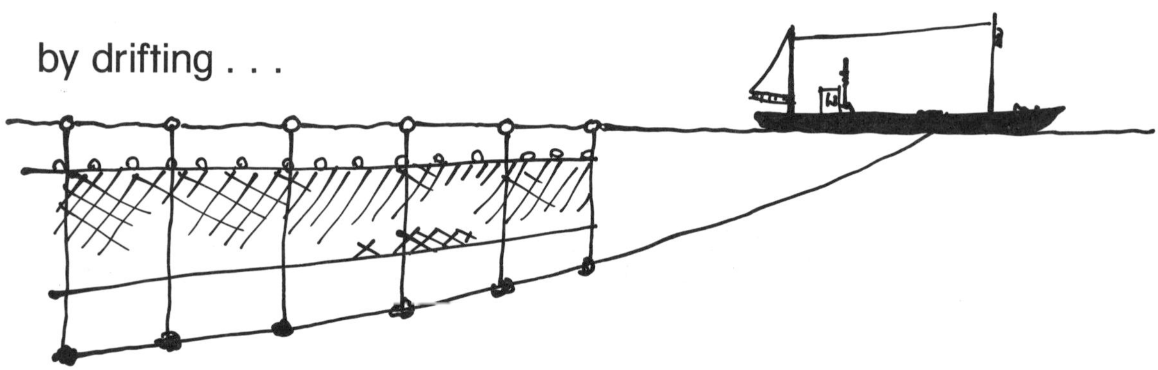

Which type of fishing is used to catch which type of fish? Stick them in the correct nets.

The long haul

On the 4th June 1966 Captain John Ridgeway and Sargeant Charles Blyth of the British Army set off in their boat *English Rose*, a 22 foot rowing boat, from Cape Cod in north America.

Ninety-one days later, on the 3rd September, they arrived in Irishmore in Ireland having rowed across the Atlantic! This was the first time in modern history that anyone had accomplished such a feat.

Fill in these two pages from the boat's log with the things you think the two men needed on their journey to keep them safe and healthy.

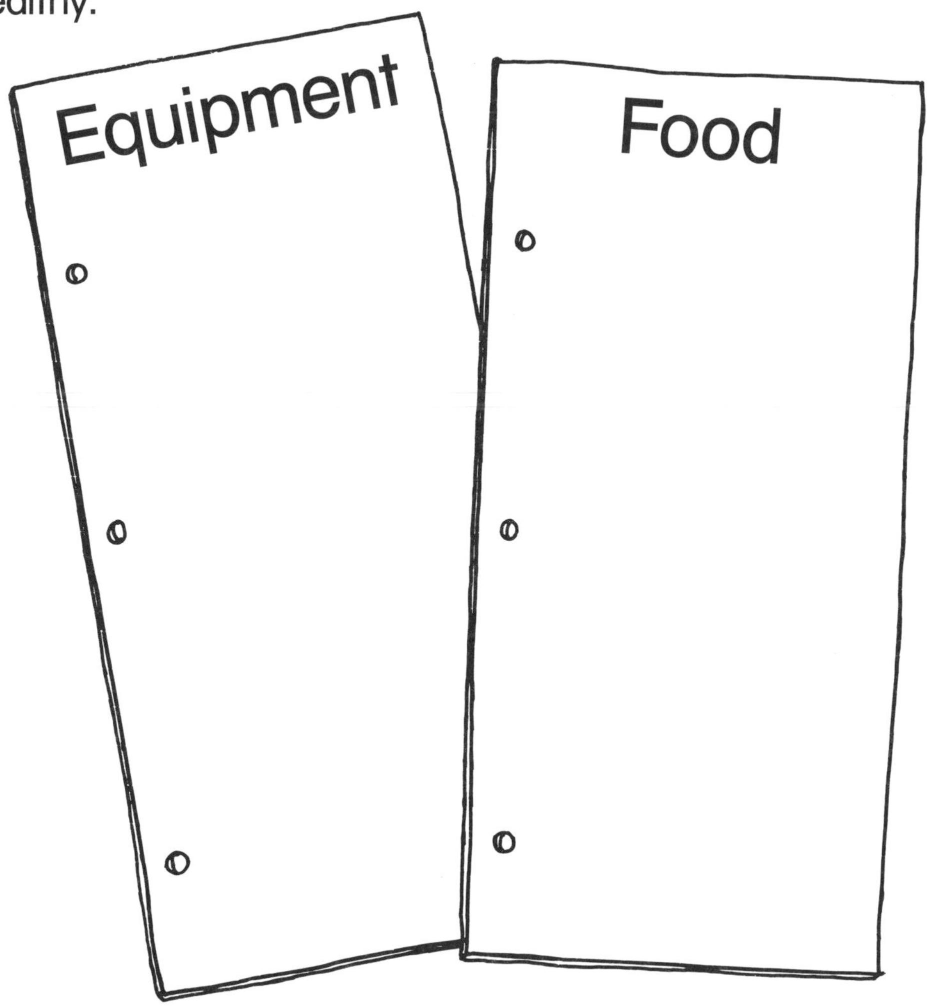

The sea today is filled with ships carrying bulky heavy cargo. What kinds of things do you think they might be carrying?

A Rollo (roll on - roll off) ship is a cargo ship that has huge opening doors in the stern of the ship. This means that all the cargo can be driven on and off the ship. This kind of ship can be loaded much quicker than a crane loaded ship; it can be back at sea with its new cargo in a very short time. Here is a list of cargo that was recently brought into the port of Grimsby by the Norwegian ship the *Norlander* . . .

Aluminium blocks, sheep's fleeces, farm implements, boat engines, plastic wrapping, and VW cars.

A stevedore is the name given to the person whose job it is to load a ship safely, so that the heavy things balance the light things and the boat sits squarely in the water.

Load the *Norlander* with its cargo . . . safely.

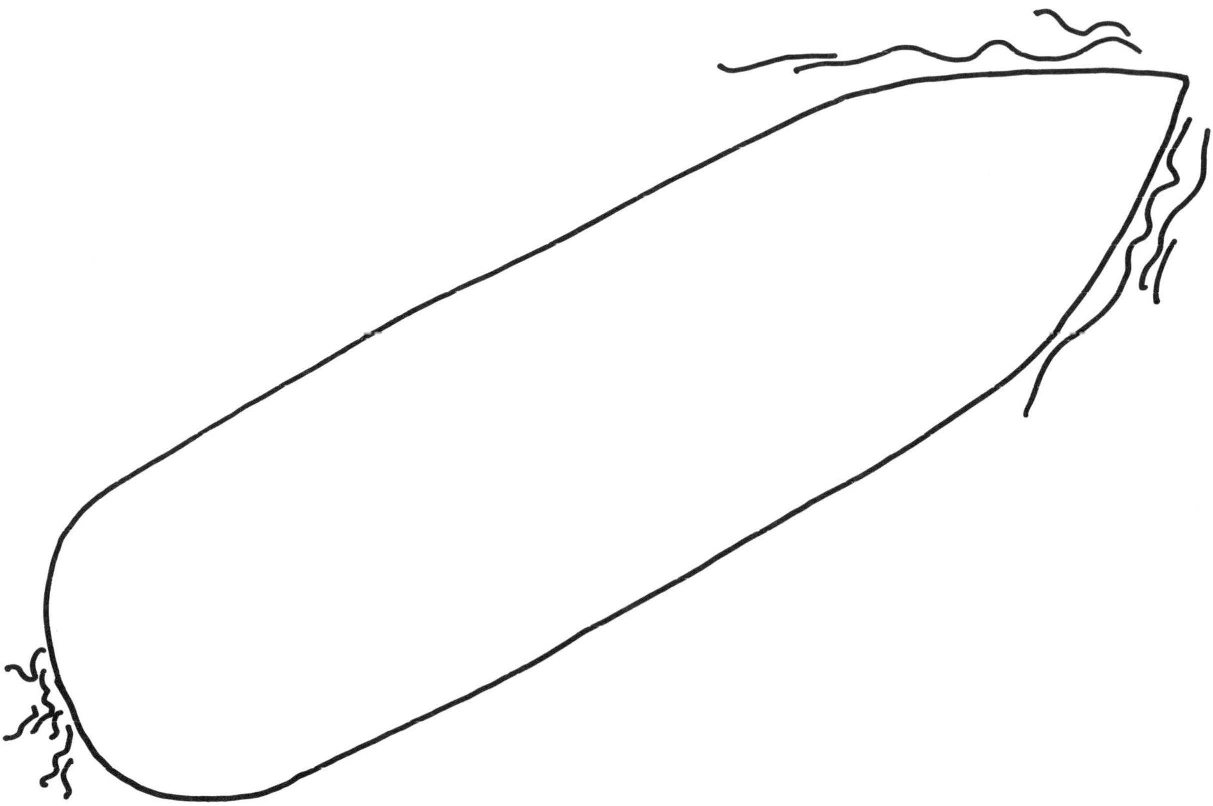

Finish the book with this Nautical Crossword!

Across
1 Ship filler
4 Francis ______
5 A Viking boat
8 Deep sea fishing boat
9 Spanish trouble!

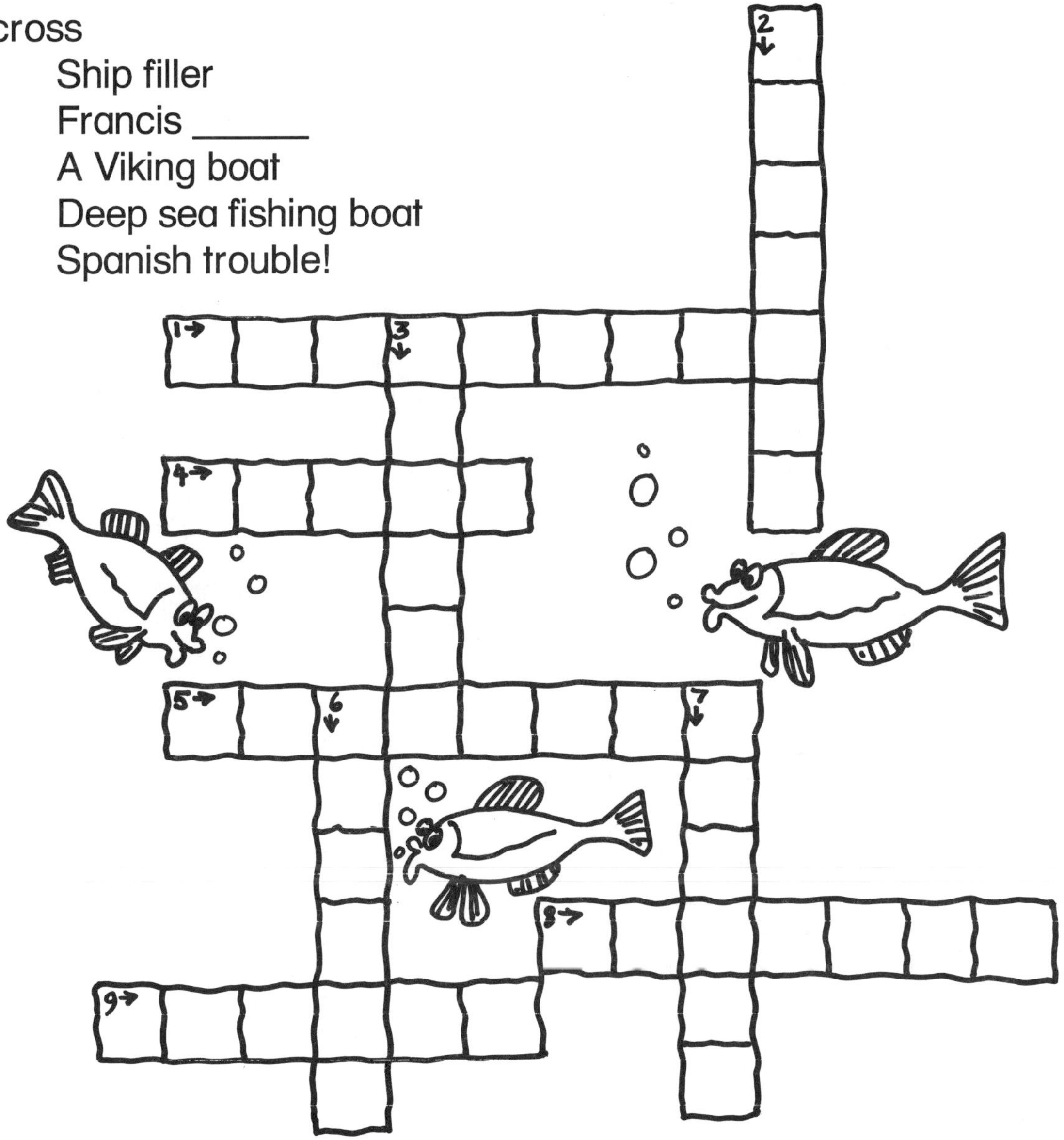

Down
2 Greek warship
3 Scandinavian sea wolf?
6 Where 3 came from
7 Raleigh could have made his chips with this!

Answers

p2 Eyes were painted on ships for good luck, and to give the ships sight! A platform was built over the cargo with planks for the crew to walk on.

p3 The pointed end was for ramming the enemy!

p4 Lines of latitude are measurement lines that run around the earth parallel with the equator. Lines of longitude are the measurement lines that run around the earth from the North Pole to the South Pole. Using the lines of latitude and longitude the seamen could calculate where they were.

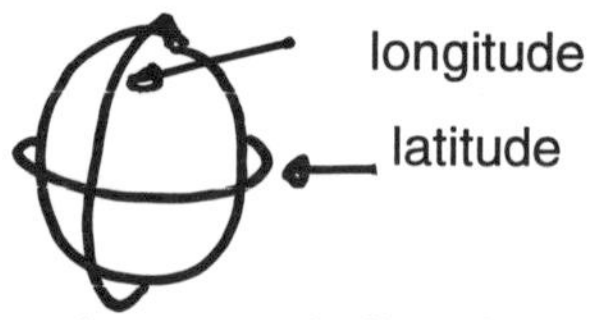

p10 The Vikings could sail their boats very close to shore and even up shallow rivers.

p11 The Vikings would use their oars when there was no wind.

p15 The *Golden Hind*

p16 Some differences are: the Tudor ship has more masts, more sails, no oars, cannons, more deck, on-board cabins.

p17 Potatoes, tobacco, sugar cane.

p18 The Spanish Armada.

p18 The musket at the top of the picture, the cannon and the thin sword, the rapier.

p20 The small boats were used to chase the whales.

p21 *Baleen* was used to make brushes and ladies' corsets; *bone* for knife handles and umbrella spokes; *blubber* for lamp oil (this was the main whale product); *ambergris* for perfume (it is still prized today and is sometimes found washed up on the beach). Plastic has replaced bone and baleen, and people no longer use oil lamps.

p23 The *Charlotte Dundas*: steam & paddle, The *Great Britain*: steam & propeller, The *Clermont*: steam, paddle & sail, The *Savannah*: steam, paddle & sail, The *Adriatic*: steam, paddle & sail.

p24 Three return journeys

p26 People fly across now!

p27 Battleship, cruiser, submarine, aircraft carrier.

p28 Trawling: cod, dab, skate, pollack, whiting. drifting: herring, shark.

p30 Check the ship is balanced i.e., doesn't have all the heavy things on one side.

p31

across		down	
1	stevedore	2	trireme
4	Drake	3	Viking
5	longship	6	Norway
8	trawler	7	potato
9	Armada		

p25

G	R	E	A	T	W	H	A	L	E	A
R				B				P		M
A				R				A		B
C				I			S	D		E
E				T			C	D		R
D	S	T	E	A	M		H	L		G
A				I			O	E		R
R				N			O			I
L	O	N	G	S	T	O	N	E		S
I			S	A	I	L	E			
N	B	L	U	B	B	E	R			
G		P	R	O	P	E	L	L	E	R

First published 1994 by Macmillan Children's Books, a division of Macmillan General Books Ltd
Cavaye Place London SW10 9PG and Basingstoke
Associated companies throughout the world

ISBN 0 330 33389 5

9 8 7 6 5 4 3 2 1

A CIP catalogue record for this book is available from the British Library.

Printed and bound in Great Britain by Henry Ling Ltd, The Dorset Press, Dorchester